Life and Survival
THE CHEETAH

Philippe Dupont

and Valérie Tracqui

FRANKLIN WATTS

in association with
TWO-CAN

In this heat the only thing to do is sleep.

These graceful impala, always on the alert, have heard something. Perhaps they sense that a cheetah is not far away.

Deep in the Savannah

The heat is overwhelming at midday. The African savannah, green and lush after the rains, stretches as far as the eye can see. Herds of gazelle graze peacefully, while zebra and antelope doze in the shade of the trees. The silence is broken only by the steady drone of insects.

Not far away lies the cheetah, scarcely visible in the long grass. He stretches and yawns: at dusk it will be time to hunt.

A big cat yawns out of hunger, not tiredness, and displays its fearsome teeth.

Four cubs means a lot of work

As the day draws on, the animals become active again. For the moment the impala have nothing to fear because the female cheetah is busy looking after her babies. She has given birth to four cubs and now she must raise them on her own.

The male and female are together for only a single day. After mating, the male leaves the female – the cubs will never know their father.

At this stage, the baby cheetahs spend all day sleeping or feeding on their mother's rich milk.

A male leopard will bring meat back to the female. Even lions have nurseries. But a female cheetah must protect her offspring, find food for them and raise them by herself. Every day she hides them in a new spot in the tall grasses, sheltering them from predators while she is away. The newborn cubs are quite helpless.

female carries one of her cubs by gripping the of its neck between her jaws.

cubs' eyes have not yet opened and they y weigh 300g (10½ ounces), no more than nall grapefruit.

A tasty meal

A brown hare rushes out of the undergrowth. It hears a sound and turns its head – too late. The hungry mother cheetah doesn't miss this opportunity and in a few bounds seizes the hare by the neck and strangles it. She then carries it back to the nest to eat it together with her cubs. The protective mother doesn't like to leave the cubs on their own for too long, so she takes just enough time to find water to drink or to hunt the small animals that pass.

The female avoids killing prey that is too big for the little cubs to eat; this hare is just the right size for them.

The mother cheetah needs energy to suckle her cubs, so she has to hunt every day. A lone cheetah only needs to hunt every two to three days.

The cheetah can go without water for up to ten days: this is essential as a source of water is not always close at hand.

10

This inquisitive cub has missed nothing.

Never let them out of sight

The days go by. The cheetah cubs are now six weeks old and extremely playful. They will jostle each other to get hold of a milky teat, and they torment their mother by climbing all over her. Sometimes she has to restore order with a swish of her paw, but usually she is very patient and will let them do as they like and lick them all over tenderly. Above all, she doesn't want to leave them, for she knows that the jackal is not far away. If she relaxes her attention, it will make a tasty meal of the cubs.

The jackal waits motionless for the right moment.

The cubs suck milk until they are two or three months old, but they supplement their diet with meat from five to six weeks after birth.

The cubs are always hungry and eat as much as they can. They have a long way to go before they are as big as their mother, who weighs 40 kg (88 pounds).

The mother cheetah licks her cub gently to reassure it.

Fortunately, the baby cheetahs are perfectly camouflaged in the savannah grasses by the thick silver mane which covers their back and head. This mop of fur will protect them until they are about two and a half months old.

"What are you doing up there? Get down at once!"

"Here I go!" You've got to be very agile to be a good hunter.

tay right here, I'm going off to hunt." The
other cheetah scans the horizon.

Learning to hunt through play

The cubs are now four months old, and the energetic young cheetahs prepare for their future as hunters against the background of the limitless dry savannah. Suddenly one of them springs into the branches of a tree. His claws are still razor-sharp. He is enjoying them while he can: in two or three months, they will be as worn as a dog's, and will be useless for climbing trees.

The young ones never seem to stop playing; they tumble about, play tag, and snap at each others' throats. But it's only for fun – these scuffles are never serious, and they take turns at being the hunter and the prey.

r the moment they can play, but soon it will be a
tter of life or death for the cubs.

Hunting is an art in itself

The mother cheetah observes a herd of peacefully grazing gazelles, and notices one of them which is a little way apart from the rest. Very slowly she crouches down, stretches her neck forward, and comes closer to the gazelle. The dry grasses help to camouflage her golden fur.

Even when they hear a small cry, the cubs obey their mother and stay together, not moving. But they watch every movement of the hunt and they are learning.

The hidden stalking can last anything from a few seconds to several hours, and requires great patience.

For the moment the Thomson's gazelles are not aware of any danger, but they would run off at full speed at the least alarm.

Suddenly the gazelles look up: have they seen anything? At once, the cheetah freezes. But they have detected nothing, and begin to graze again. The mother cheetah sets off once more, taking great care. She must get as close as possible to her prey, so she hides herself in the long grasses, slipping behind a hummock, then behind a dead tree trunk, and finally behind a bush.

This gazelle seems younger and weaker than the others.

Luckily, the wind hasn't borne the cheetah's scent to the gazelle and she is now close enough to her prey to be sure of capturing it. A cheetah's hunt ends in failure twice out of every three attempts.

The cheetah is the fastest mammal on Earth, reaching an incredible 100 km (62 miles) per hour at top speed. But it runs out of breath quickly, and is unable to keep up this pace over long distances.

Fast as lightning

The cheetah has to come out of hiding about 50 m (164 feet) from the gazelle. She starts at a trot. By the time the herd has been alerted to the danger, the cheetah is less than 30 m (98 feet) away. As the gazelles scatter, the cheetah quickens her pace. She begins to run in a succession of huge bounds, and almost seems to be flying. As she draws near, the gazelle zigzags sharply, trying to throw off its attacker. But the cheetah is supple: she twists and turns in pursuit, using her long tail to keep her balance when changing direction.

At last the cheetah has managed to knock the gazelle off its feet with a blow of her paw on its flank. This is the end of the chase and now the cheetah seizes her prey by the throat and keeps her jaws firmly clenched.

A cheetah's jaws are not powerful enough to inflict a fatal bite, so it must seize its prey's throat in exactly the right place, to strangle it within a few minutes – a difficult but deadly effective method.

Something to get their teeth into

The mother cheetah has scarcely killed her victim before her sharp little call is the signal for her starving youngsters to come to her. They have watched her closely, despite the distance, and they respond at once to her summons. With a last burst of effort, the cheetah drags her prey into a sheltered spot, hidden in the tall grasses. The cubs want to eat immediately, but their exhausted mother lies panting for a quarter of an hour.

She looks around anxiously: there's no time to lose. As soon as she has caught her breath, she tears hungrily into her meal, starting at the nourishing rump; the cubs follow suit.

When her cubs were still young, the cheetah could feed them on young gazelles which were easy to catch, but now she has to hunt bigger prey.

"Let's have a bite of this animal while Mummy gets her breath back. Isn't it tough!"

20

An adult cheetah will eat almost 3 kg (6½ pounds) of fresh meat daily. What is left over will be eaten by the other carnivores of the savannah.

The hyena is already on its way, attracted by the smell. The cheetahs have hardly finished their meal before they have to give way to this powerful predator. Soon, jackals and vultures will pick the carcass clean.

After the cheetahs have done all the hard work, hyenas, lions, and sometimes even leopards and hunting dogs will come to steal their food.

All four cubs are still alive. Often, two out of three cubs will die of disease or be killed by a predator.

Family life

The well-fed youngsters grow up quickly and learn to carry themselves proudly. But they must still stay together as a family for many months, until they are able to hunt for themselves.

Defending territory takes skill, particularly when you're on your own. Some cheetahs are killed in bloody and vicious fights. It can sometimes be better to stick together in a group, both to provide defence and to bring down larger prey. Several cheetahs working in this way can capture hartebeests, topi, kob or kudu. On occasions a team of cheetahs will even be so daring as to attack young zebras or small gnus. But usually they lead a nomadic existence, and must stay on the move constantly in pursuit of the wandering herds.

Once they are independent, the males sometimes fight over territory. They will mark their boundaries with scratch marks on the bark of trees, piles of dung or squirts of urine.

This young cheetah is not joking when he bares his teeth. The intention of the scuffles between brothers and sisters is to become ever more agile, supple and speedy.

Leaving home

The young cheetahs have been practising their hunting methods for some months. They have lost their silver manes, and it's time for them to show what they can do. Their tussles become fiercer and the time for playing is over. The cheetahs bite at each others' throats and roll around in the dust, but they always seem to know when to stop: nothing serious happens between brothers and sisters.

Now the mother cheetah brings down young gazelles or warthogs for them. She is content to keep an eye on her cubs from a distance. Time goes past until one day, when it is the mating season once more, the mother cheetah is attracted by another male. She goes off with him, leaving her almost fully-grown offspring to make their own way in the harsh world.

Today is the big day: the cheetahs will go off, each in a different direction. While the two brothers join another band of bachelor males, their sister will remain alone. The young cheetahs are now a year and a half old, and their family life is finally over.

No rest for the cheetah

The cheetah is vulnerable. It has many natural enemies, more powerful and better organised than itself. Even in the national parks where it is a protected species, tourists come and disturb it. What can be done to save this champion sprinter?

The competition
The cheetah lacks the strength and boldness with which to defend its recently killed prey. Little by little, lions are forcing the cheetah to live in regions of the savannah with rougher ground or with too little cover. In such cases, the cheetah finds it hard to hunt as its technique is not effective in these conditions.

Fearless tourists will come so close to a cheetah that it has no opportunity to hunt in its usual way.

The nervous cheetah finds it hard to eat its fill, as even a flock of vultures attracted by the carcass can make it flee.

The tourists
Used by mankind for thousands of years in hunting, the cheetah is almost extinct in Asia. It has also become extremely rare in Africa, where it has found sanctuary in the national parks. Even here, the cheetah is unable to hunt in peace. Tourists' vehicles cause prey to run off, so the cheetah is forced to hunt during the hottest part of the day. But the heat is tiring and more hunts end in failure.

Scientists have fitted a radio collar around this cheetah's neck so that they can follow it from area to area using a reception aerial and learn more about its way of life.

Protection

A team of scientists in Tanzania is researching into the cheetah's behavioural patterns and needs, to provide it with effective protection. A starving cheetah will sometimes kill domestic animals, which has naturally made it unpopular. The protectors of the cheetah are therefore trying to make it more accepted by the local community. The future of this splendid creature now depends upon special game reserves where the presence of other carnivores and tourists is controlled and restricted.

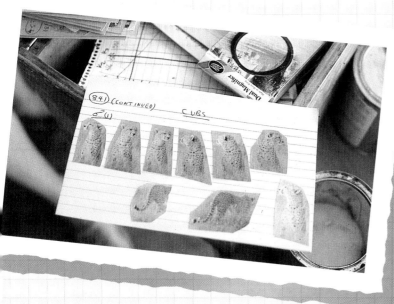

ch individual cheetah has its own record rd. To distinguish between them, aracteristic marks are noted down for each imal: the number of black rings along the l, any marks behind the ears, and so forth.

The spotted cat family

The cheetah, the leopard, the jaguar, the serval and the ocelot are all members of the spotted cat family. They are similar to the domestic cat and are all superb hunters. Their movements are agile, supple and quiet, while their graceful bodies and beautiful markings serve to camouflage them against the surrounding scenery. What else do they have in common? They are all under threat of extinction from being hunted for their skins.

Let's look at each one in turn.

▲ The *leopard*, or *panther*, has shorter legs tha the cheetah, and is more heavy-set. It likes to rest in trees to eat its prey. It mostly hunts at night, by ambushing its victims: after locating the prey, the leopard leaps upon it. The leopard has ring-shaped spots and striking green eyes.

▶ The *serval*, a much smaller animal, can be recognised by its huge ears and short tail. It has long legs and its spots fall in a pattern of stripes: in some regions, it has no spots at all. The serval lives in Africa, near water or where there is plenty of vegetation. It weighs between 6 and 15 kg (13–33 pounds), which is very light compared to the 60–115 kg (132–253½ pounds) of a jaguar.

▲ The *jaguar* is very similar to the leopard, except that it is even more heavily-built, with a noticeably larger head and bigger paws. Its ring-shaped spots are also broader. But above all, it is difficult to confuse them as, unlike the leopard or the cheetah which inhabit Africa and Asia, the jaguar lives only in the jungles of Central and South America.

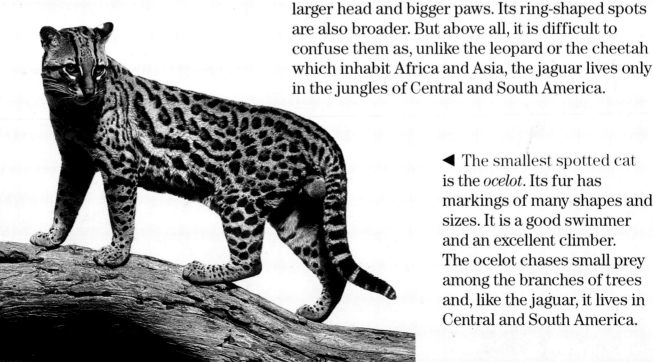

◀ The smallest spotted cat is the *ocelot*. Its fur has markings of many shapes and sizes. It is a good swimmer and an excellent climber. The ocelot chases small prey among the branches of trees and, like the jaguar, it lives in Central and South America.

INDEX

First published in this edition in 1990 by
Franklin Watts
96 Leonard Street
London EC2A 4RH

French edition © Editions Milan 1989, 300 rue Léon-Joulin 31101, Cedex 100, France
English edition © Two-Can Publishing Ltd 1990, 27 Cowper Street, London EC2A 4AP
English translation by Monica Byles

A CIP Cataloguing record for this book is available from the British Library ISBN 0-7496-0373-9

Printed in Belgium by Casterman, SA

Photo credits:
JACANA: Arthur Bertrand p 8 (bottom), p 9 (bottom), p 12 (bottom), p 13, p 14, p 16 (top), p 17 (top), p 20, p 21 p 24, p 26-27; Varin. Visage p 25 (top); Denis Huot p 8 (top), p 25 (bottom); Degré p 11; Cordier p 28 (bottom), Robert p 10, Gohier p 29 (bottom); GUERRIER: p 12 (top), p 15 (top), p 16 (bottom), p 26 (bottom); TRACQUI: p 17 (bottom); GUENOT: p 21 (bottom); DENIS-HUOT: p 27 (top right, bottom left); ZIESLER: p 4, p 6-7 (background) p 18 (top left and middle), p 15 (bottom), p 7 (right); NATURE: Polking: p 6 (top), p 19 (bottom right), p 22-23, Gohier p 29 (top); DARMON: p 28 (top)